MGTOW

men going their own way

10

things

men don't do anymore

Elaine
FLOWERS

Published by:
Before You Publish – Book Press
Addison, Texas

Cover Designs:
In House at Before You Publish – Book Press
Edits:
EBM Professional Services

Published and printed in the United States of
America
Copyright © 2017 Elaine Garcia

First Edition
ISBN-13: 978-0-9747388-2-6
ISBN-10: 0-9747388-2-4

Printed in the United States of America

Flowers, Elaine
M.G.T.O.W.: 10 Things Men Don't Do Anymore –
First Edition

Blog responses posted on HubPages.com and PairedLife.com.

What's most important in life reveals itself only in its absence.

- Albert Einstein

Larry
38 hours ago
At 55 I no longer pursue women and have chosen to go MGTOW. I can't honestly think of a relationship I've been in where having a woman in my life has actually made it better. I miss sex, but really, it isn't worth the nonsense that goes along with it.

MGTOW
men going their own way

10

things

men don't do anymore

Elaine
FLOWERS

BeforeYouPublish Book Press™
—— We Publish Books ——

ADDISON, TEXAS

MGTOW: 10 Things Men Don't Do Anymore

- Contents -

Foreword: By Brian W. Smith

Introduction: MGTOW

FINALLY: 10 Things Women Could Do Better

Foreword

Let's face it, times have changed. Snow in Louisiana has become the norm. Reality television stars are more popular than trained actors. And the roles of men and women in relationships have changed drastically.

Nowhere is this relationship shift more apparent than in the dating arena. Who should extend the invitation? Who should pay for the meal? Who should drive? These questions, that two decades were relationship no-brainers, have become the talking points for heated gender debates, and the basis for this unique *relationship* book.

When Elaine first told me she was writing this book, I wasn't sold on the idea. *Just what the world needs, another male bashing book*, was my initial sarcastic thought. But, my viewpoint changed a few weeks ago after I witnessed two couples interacting at a shopping mall.

While sitting in my car, I spotted a young couple coming out of a department store holding hands. The woman wore a smile that spanned the width of her face. A lovesick gaze, the type that probably inspired the heart-eyed emoji, could be seen from across the parking lot. Her male companion, on the other hand, didn't seem as enamored with the woman or the moment.

The young man, whose pants sagged below his

butt and unkempt afro looked like a bad wig, stared at his cell phone as if nothing else in the world mattered—to include the beautiful woman craning her neck and pawing at his chin in an effort to get his attention.

As the couple approached the rear of their car, I was not surprised to see how things unfolded. The young man released her hand, entered the car from the driver side, and sat behind the steering wheel—eyes still glued to his cell phone—while the woman stood outside in the stiff breeze. It took a rap on the tinted windshield and her calling his name while waving mockingly, before he unlocked her door.

Damn millennials, I thought and shook my head in disgust. I rolled my eyes and mumbled, "I don't know what's worse: his lack of chivalry or her willingness to tolerate it."

Moments later, I watched an older couple walk toward the department store. In hindsight, I should have viewed the man's decision to walk in front of the woman as a red flag, but I didn't. Instead, I ignored his faux pas and assumed his gray hair was an indicator he knew better—I was wrong. The man opened the door, entered the store, and didn't bother to look back at his female acquaintance.

"Damn, it's not just a millennial problem. Even older men are rude to their women," I mumbled.

As disturbing as my observations in the parking lot were, they made me realize something—courting women is a lost art. Fortunately, I understand the difference between a *symptom* and an *ailment*. The inability to court a woman is a *symptom*. The shift in gender roles is the *ailment*.

When I was a young sergeant in the U.S. Army I was taught, supervisors need to understand that people *respect* what you *inspect*. It's a lesson I feel every person—man and woman—should learn and apply it to their dating life. When you don't set standards and hold people accountable to those standards, respect for your standards dissipates and chaos prevails. When it comes to dating, women have lowered their dating standards, and the response from a lot of men is as to be expected—mediocre.

In "Men Going Their Own Way: 10 Things Men Don't Do Anymore," Elaine Flowers has pointed out the problem while capturing the anger, confusion, stubbornness, and passion of hundreds of men. Their perspectives are enlightening, disturbing, and create the type of heartfelt discussions that break down barriers and forge understanding. This is not only a good read—it's a must-read.

Brian W. Smith
Bestselling author of twenty novels, including "Glass Houses," "Nina's Got a Secret," "Quagmire," and the "Sleepy Carter Mystery Series." When Brian is not writing or touring, he serves as an Adjunct Professor of Creative Writing at both Collin College and Dallas Community College. A native of New Orleans, LA., Brian is currently living in McKinney, TX.

Introduction

MGTOW — Men Going Their Own Way is a movement. Yes, it's a thing!

What does it mean? It means that men are fed up with women getting over on them. Or, at least that's how some of them see it. I would never dream of speaking on this from the male perspective, but what I do know is that because of MGTOW, there are at least ten things that men just don't do anymore.

I discovered this new phenomena after writing a blog titled, "Dating: 10 Things Men Don't Do Anymore" and a guy who left a comment enlightened me. Yep, ladies, we've done it now. Men are resisting and they're resisting in a way that is shocking.

Even though I consider myself an independent woman, I'm not on the feminism bandwagon professing to be equal to men. I mean, we're equal as humans go, but there are many things that differentiate the two sexes. There are plenty of things that a woman cannot do that a man can and vice versa. I don't think, behave, or operate like a man and I'm not interested in the man who wants to think, behave, or operate like a woman.

With that in mind, the concept of men going their own way is a new expression by men in their 20s and 30s who are not interested in building a life with a woman. It is easy to see how men arrived at this station when many of them believe that they come out on the short end of the stick when a marriage or long-term relationship dissolves. I happen to believe just the opposite but I won't argue with how others see it.

My concern, or at least one of them, is if men are no longer interested in building a relationship with a woman, what options are left? And what will all of this look like long term? It makes sense if sex is the only thing a woman is good for, then yes, there are alternatives. But I would like to think that men know women have more to offer than a good lay.

So, if you think I am making this whole thing up—Men Going Their Own Way—read further and take a look at the ten things that men no longer do.

(just a few) BLOG RESPONSES

Simon
6 weeks ago
Find me a good woman who saves physical intimacy for a man who truly deserves her and I'll happily go to the ends of the earth to impress her.

sigma1932
5 days ago
It's ridiculous to expect men to bring a solid core of traditional masculine strength (which is what you listed in this article, Elaine) unless you're going to provide equal full-stop traditional feminine value in return...

ban
2 months ago
I've come up with my list of 10 things that women do not do any more.
1 - Women will never tell you whose child you are raising
2 - Women do not keep their families together
3 - Women are not forgiving
4 - Women do not cook
5 - Women do not partner with strong masculine and moral men
6 - Women do not contribute to the household expenses
7 - Women have no shame
8 - Women do not work
9 - Women do not take care of their children
10 - Women are not loving
It's no wonder why men now are doing their own thing for themselves and excluding selfish, self-centered women behind.

Marty Frazier
2 weeks ago
Great article Elaine!
The one thing I find is that it seems women don't know how to be courted this way anymore. I'm 33 and all of your stuff seems normal for a date, but women just aren't into one on one dates anymore. I brought a flower on a date before. My date awkwardly accepted it but later told her friend, whom I work with, that "he gave me a flower thinking I'd sleep with him on the first date". That was not even my intention at all.

Siv Ingrid
6 days ago
I am a woman, but I am just thinking loud on behalf of the men here. If I was expected to initiate every single date I went on, and even pay for every expense (gifts and all) then all these dates, that may or may not turn out well, it would end up being quite costly to maintain, right? I do think the dating culture in the US differs quite a bit from where I live (I live in Norway).

Nunya99
2 months ago
Men are sick of being ATM machines for women. They get criticized and abused and accused of all kinds of crap. They are sick of it and you can blame nobody but yourselves. Women in their twenties will screw anything that moves and cheat on any man no matter how good he is. You have nothing to offer us you don't love us and you don't care about us so why should we care about you?

10 things

men don't do anymore

#10

Men don't ask women on dates anymore

"I've had a wonderful time tonight!"

#10 Men don't ask women on dates anymore

They're called "Meet Ups" now. WTH?
Online is how many people find and date each other. So, it makes great sense to meet that someone new in a public place. No problem there. But what happens when this is not the first time getting together? The common practice of "meet ups" have replaced real dating. Guys request to "meet up" with their date at a location to hang out as opposed to actually picking her up to take her out.

If two people are unfamiliar with each other, the ability to cut the date short and get the heck out of Dodge is what is needed. So, meet ups, in that case, work wonderfully. But as a regular date practice—come on now. That is, simply, not wanting to put in any effort.

Lazy: men only want to come over...
What has now happened, however, is that the fellas have become lazy when it comes to all dates. Becoming lazy is not due to any inadequacies, it is because men no longer find women worth the effort it takes to plan and execute a date. If the man's goal is to lay up with the woman, why mess around with all the pesky details leading up to it, and just start

where they want to end up? And since meet ups are now the norm, women are used to this poor exhibition and allow it. Yes, I blame it all on women. Women have not only allowed this, they have lowered their own behaviors to make men not even bother treating them like ladies.

Waiting on a woman to ask him out...
There is a community of shy guys (I'll call them) that don't bother to ask a woman out because they're waiting on the women to ask them. Yes, this guy needs the woman to make the first move (and then the second and so on). Not only is he waiting on her to show the initial interest, he wants her to ask him out, and then plan and sometimes pay. I'm not making this up or just being rude—this really happens. Oh, and there are women subscribing. So, if he's happy with a woman being in charge moving forward, and doesn't care that he'll feel like a little boy, and know that his woman is going to now be his mother, and his woman/mother will be making the decisions, and... I think you get the picture. Dude, grow a pair.

Turd Ferguson
3 months ago
Wow, sounds like you're really the lazy one. Men need to do this or that just to have the small chance that your entitled ass won't brush him aside once the next guy comes along. The problem with this type of article is that it passes blame on everyone else instead of examining the facts. How about you come pick me up, bring me a gift, buy me a drink, pay

for my dinner, and then I can choose whether I want a second date with you?

Javed
14 months ago
Men don't ask women out anymore: It's all right, just put your princess mentality aside and you ask them out. What's the big deal here? Don't get frustrated and try to live with it.

Steve
89 minutes ago
I went out on a date last week with a girl who asked me out, which I thought was quite exciting. We're both in our early 30s.
The first words out of her mouth were, "I don't really need a man" (not the best start on a date!) followed by lots of rambling about how much of a strong, independent woman she was and could do everything for herself and how lonely she was and wanted a boyfriend.
I think lots of women have taken to the feminist teachings so hard that they can't even date anymore, as they see it as some sort of surrender. She really wanted a boyfriend but wanted to prove she didn't need me at the same time, as if we were in some sort of competition to prove who was the most alpha, so strange. Needless to say, I won't be seeing her again and that may be my last foray into the dating world for a bit if all women are like that… Internet porn is looking very attractive.

#9

Men don't ask women out in advance anymore

"Tonight's the night!"

#9 Men don't ask women out in advance anymore

Women accept it...

Now when women actually accept a date, there's barely enough time for her to do the necessary date-prep work.

Is it because men are procrastinators? Is it that men are busy and being in the company of a woman is the last thing on their minds? Is it that men have little or no consideration for a woman's plans or her schedule? Or is it even that women no longer require a man to give them advance notice to go out with them?

I am going to go with the latter. Because date requests rarely come in, women jump at the chance to go on one, therefore accepting a dinner invitation moments before her suitor is available to take her. She accepts because she's afraid he won't ask again, moreover, who knows how long it will be before anyone else will either.

He doesn't want the woman to think she's a priority...

There is another group of men who want to keep a woman in her place, so to speak. He doesn't want a woman to think she's special (especially if she's not special to him), so he treats her as if she was a last option. And there are women who actually go along with this program—they go along, to get along, thinking any date is better than no date at all.

By treating a woman as if she isn't a priority, this starts a slow conditioning process, which ultimately has a woman accepting whatever a man dishes out. Giving a woman the impression she is not a priority is a control tactic. And keeping a woman unsure is the goal of a man who fears being the one who is unsure in the relationship. An insecure person fears being vulnerable or giving up his or her power.

Men don't know any better...

There are some men (certainly men in their 20s) who just don't know any better and part of the reason they don't is because women no longer require advance notice, and certainly don't request it. And some don't know any better because they haven't witnessed it being done.

The problem is, women who have had the fortunate experience of being treated well by men, just can't accept the BS that goes on with today's dating scene. Things that were once taken for granted are now just memories, and sometimes those things are all together forgotten because the nonsense seems to be the status quo. Yes, men haven't been taught how to date a woman so it is now normal for women to accept it.

###

Someone who just plays video games
3 months ago
I just don't care because I'm having far
too much fun enjoying everything in my
life to even imagine the thought of
sharing it with someone else, and
besides the media doesn't do women
justice with the amount of shit they do
to make men fear like they have to
sacrifice their own enjoyment just to
make you feel happy, we're not into you
because you cannot do the same for us.

Don F1212
2 months ago
We cannot turn back time. Men, nor
women, can cherry pick what they want to
keep and what the want to bring back in
today's time. We keep trying, hoping,
praying, blogging but it can't be done
or it would have been by now. Men can't
have women act as the women of
generations ago. Women can't have men
act as the men of generations ago.

#8

Men don't take charge of dating plans anymore

"...I don't know; what do you want to do?"

#8 Men don't take charge of dating plans anymore

Not interested in being a champion...
"Hey, so what do you want to do?"
"I don't know; what do you want to do?"
"I don't care; what do you want to do?"
The never-ending exchange...
There are few things more frustrating than when you finally decide to go out with a guy and he leaves all the decisions up to you. Not only is he showing his lack of real interest in showing you a good time, he's running the risk of you going over his budget for the evening. Besides, women love it when a man takes charge, but at the same time is open to her opinion.

Even the woman who is a control freak wants a date that can, not only make a decision, but will, in fact, implement that decision.

Fear of failure...
I used to believe being a champion was in the male DNA. Now, I'm not so sure. Now, something as simple as taking charge of date plans, and as complex as being head of household and taking charge of family plans, seems to be foreign to men. Not only foreign, but something they simply do not

desire. Even if men know that extending simple gestures make them appealing to women, or even champions, they are not interested.

They don't have to...
Even women who would love for a guy to take charge of dating plans find themselves accepting the lack of effort. These women have given up and given in. Either that, or they're just so happy to finally get a date. Sadly, some women don't think they should have expectations and will not only take charge of dating plans, they have even convinced themselves that it is okay to propose marriage. But, I digress... let's get back to dating.

Alpha
4 months ago
I can't believe what I've just read! I think you need to get over yourself, you women wanted equality but expect us to do everything. Times have changed how about you women do some of the things you have mentioned in your little rant.

Realist
2 years ago
… the real reason to this problem is: Online dating and overweight women! Since online has an abundant of fatties, men have learned to settle… These women are less work and willing to give more than their prettier counterparts. Ever been on a date with a fatty? They have no problem going Dutch… Hell, they have no problem paying for the whole date!

#7

Men don't show up with a gift/token anymore

"A little something for you."

He's never heard of it...

It was most likely in the 1950s (and before) when this was common practice. However, I've dated in the 70s, 80s, and the 90s and even though some of my dates showed up empty handed, it was not unheard of to have one with flowers, a teddy bear, or something ready to hand over when I opened the door. In fact, the last time it actually happened was in the late 90s.

I don't think it's necessary for this to happen all of the time but what saddens me is that there are some young men who have never heard of even doing this. And sadly, that means there are some young ladies who would never experience or expect it. The point is, a guy seriously interested in a particular girl should go the extra mile when trying to impress her, and this is the perfect way to get started.

An added and unnecessary expense...

Yes, it is an extra expense and it may even seem unnecessary. But a token that could be free or cost very little, could go a really long way with a woman. Frankly, it shows forethought, consideration, and class. In an instance where a woman is leaning towards indifference to her date, a simple gesture will redirect her feelings.

It's corny...

For every guy who thinks standing at a woman's door holding a teddy bear is corny, I'll show you a guy missing out. Confidence is all that's needed and the fear of appearing corny while trying to please his date will disappear. The secure man knows there is nothing corny about putting a smile on a woman's face.

Omari Valentine
5 weeks ago
If you transported a guy who did all of these things from the 1950s, he would get chewed up and spit out by the dating scene today.

Bruno
16 months ago
Men, after reasonable consideration of the situation conclude that dealing with women offer no advantage, no return, no enjoyment. Quite the contrary: women are mostly boring, demanding, whiny, wimpy and most of them, so ugly that I actually am considering chemical castration to stop the pain of having useless sexual desire.

#6

Men don't work at impressing anymore

"Looking good!"

#6 Men don't work at impressing anymore

MGTOW...

Is it perhaps that winning the hearts of women is not worth their effort? The goal, when impressing a woman, is to win her heart, ultimately to land in marital bliss. When the so-called bliss turns into a nightmare and he's splitting half his earnings, at the very least, down the middle, it leaves him wondering why he even went there. And this is where we get to MGTOW (Men Going Their Own Way). Ouch!

If a man doesn't want to get married, why would he put in a lot of effort, time, and money to win the heart of a woman? And that's the question of the century.

Some men believe women should be working to impress them...

Something happened with the media advancement of today's age and the need for men to impress women. Notwithstanding all of the superficial things women do to enhance their looks to get a man's attention, men now seem to be under the assumption that women should only work at impressing them. I'm sure there are many places to point the finger but women have been tricked into thinking that they are supposed to be working at the pleasure of men in the virtual world, and in real life. What happened to men working to prove that they are worthy and capable of being with a woman? Something is definitely wrong here.

Women just aren't worth it...

It was bound to happen. Women have taken advantage of being the so-called weaker sex long enough and men are no longer with that program. The current movement of younger men is not falling under what they see as a trap. The trap that men of prior generations to them fell for: paying for everything during a marriage and losing everything in a divorce. I get it. I honestly do. But it leaves me wondering what the alternative for these same men will be. If they are not interested in marriage, are they at least interested in a loving relationship with a woman? What will this look like in the grand scheme of things? Are men and women no longer coupling?

Sadly, in a struggle to understand, there are more questions than answers.

Contradict
3 months ago
Feminism. Don't bitch about what you guys created. It's your fault.

Kylesar1
17 months ago
Your #6 point: We have to prove we're worthy of being with a woman? The

counter question is what about you is worth having to prove my worth to be with you? In other words, men nowadays are asking, "what do you bring to the table?" Women can't seem to really answer this question, yet expect the man to prove THEIR worth to them. Why in the blue hell should I prove myself to be with someone who doesn't bring a thing to the table?

#5

Men don't give meaningful compliments anymore

"You are such a sweet and caring woman."

#5 Men don't give meaningful compliments anymore

Men fail to see the benefit...

A man whistling or giving a catcall when a woman walks by is nothing new. But that's not what I'm talking about here. I'm referring to men ONLY taking notice of a woman's physical attributes. And I'm not referring to locker room jargon, either. Men seem to be less and less interested in a woman's heart—her spirituality—her core values, hence, him only showing appreciation for what's on the outside.

Men don't want to build their women up in a meaningful way...

Fear she may start thinking highly of herself keeps some men from building his woman up. I'll go as far as calling it borderline emotional abuse. Only the man who doesn't think much of himself would make a conscious effort to make sure his woman doesn't think much of herself.

He is too busy looking at himself to notice his woman...

Let's face it. There are men (and not just metro-sexual men) that are self-involved. These men are too concerned with what makes them happy to take notice of anyone else's wants or needs, let alone a potential date's wants or needs. Yes, there are signs of gender roles flip-flopping and I find it disturbing.

Francisco
2 months ago
I'm not trying to hurt anyone; I'm trying to be 100% honest with you. But why would an attractive man like to be a provider these days, what would we get in exchange? ...And anyway ...women probably know they are getting old, and know they now have [fewer] options than before. Remember I'm not trying to offend, just being honest. But let me tell you, we men are seeing the game here. Taking care of a woman for the rest of your life is quite a sacrifice... even bigger if the woman is not attractive anymore. We don't receive anything from that deal.

#4

Men don't ask women to dance anymore

"Can I have this dance?"

#4 Men don't ask women to dance anymore

Fear of rejection...

You're at a club, or even a private party, and unlike back in the day when there were couples, there are now groups of women on the dance floor and men standing on the sidelines, either ogling them or ignoring them all together. Now, if a woman doesn't ask a man to dance, she's stuck with not dancing at all or only getting off the wall to do the Wobble with a group of other women. Men don't ask. Is it really the end of the world if a woman says no? It's just a dance. No one likes rejection; I get that. But these new-age men seem to take it so personally.

He's shy...

Being shy is only attractive for so long. Guys, get over it. You're self-conscious? Get over it. The same way you believe a woman is sizing you up, she's thinking that you're doing the same thing to her. So, bite the bullet. Take one for the team. Get over yourself and make a move.

Video age: would rather watch women dance than join them...

This is the age of voyeurism. People in general are in a habit of watching other's lives play out publicly while choosing not to have one of their own. If it's not a reality show addiction, it is a social media addiction where they are keeping up with some stranger's daily activities. And now, no one knows how to interact with one another in person, e.g., asking a woman to dance.

you lost me
4 months ago
Yeah I used to do all of these things, and women lambasted, berated, and rejected me for them. I consistently lost to the meth dealer with washboard abs, or the Eminem wannabe, or the guy who parties and drinks all the time... enjoy your cats ladies, I'm gone forever.

Happiness
6 hours ago
Elaine Flowers,
They don't make the type of man you are describing anymore. Only very few left. It's called old school with class, such as High quality; admirable style; cachet. I would go back with you but we can't so we just have to make the best with the present, and then who knows what future brings?

Timmy
8 months ago
My sisters have similar gripes... I understand the purpose of your article, and ask you to pardon my deviation... I

miss the older days where there was a wonderful interchange of leader and follower in dance of romance. But with men expected to be leaders (in the appropriate situations, say dating) and women now told to be leaders (not bad guidance but clumsily given, and fed with a disdain for men rather than self respect…) too many toes stepped on. A man learns this in dancing, to lead you must first master following, no place better or worse, just stop complaining and dance for gods sake.

#3 Men don't buy drinks anymore

He doesn't know what it means to be a gentleman...
Not only are women *not* being asked to dance, men don't offer to buy a woman a drink anymore. However, they have no problem taking up her time talking while sipping on theirs. Obituary: Chivalry is so unbelievably dead.

Wasted money...
Some men use the excuse that it is a waste of money to buy a woman a drink with the chances of there being nothing to ultimately gain. A drink? Really? If $10 will set you back, stay home.

Not his date...
This goes along with wasted money. Why buy a woman a drink when you're not on a date with her? Again, it's just a drink. Do you want to talk to her? Are you interested? Do you want to have a reason to stick around and chat it up? I'm not talking about a man offering to buy a drink to every woman he runs across at a bar or in a club. But if he finds a certain woman appealing, what's the big deal?

dashingscorpio
2 years ago
Personally speaking, even back in the 80s, I never bought women drinks in a club and if I felt like I was "taking up her time" I moved on.

catrina
3 years ago
Say it again, girl... don't even get me started. I could add a few more to this list... think these are a few of the reasons women are staying single longer. Most of us can do without this nonsense.

damien modern
2 years ago
Id rather set my money on fire than use it to buy a woman a drink on first meeting. In fact, just for giggles I have done just that-a woman asked me to buy her a drink, I pulled out a $10 note and moved as if to order her a drink, then changed my mind and set it on fire. The look on her face-priceless. If, after meeting a woman and talking for a while, and she's charming and the spark is there, then, maybe.

Insidious Sid
2 years ago
Why men are not doing these things anymore? Feminism has been beating these things OUT OF US for FORTY YEARS! And besides, you can't have CHIVALRY *and* FEMINISM. It's one-way or the other. I don't mean men need to be nasty to women

for women to be equal, I am saying for women to choose equality they also must lose the special privileges associated with being female.

#2

Men don't make phone calls anymore

"Good morning, beautiful!"

#2 Men don't make phone calls anymore

The age of texting...

I am all about modern technology but not to the chagrin of authentic communication. Texting is not a way to get to know someone. Texting is for, "I'm on my way," "I'm running late," not for, "What kind of work do you do?" and "Tell me about yourself." Everyone being short on time and wanting to microwave his or her interactions has reduced us to this format of engagement and it just doesn't work.

He's lazy...

Some men are busy and simply do not have time to phone jockey, hugged up with a cell phone until the wee hours of the morning. But he will do all of that and more if he is genuinely interested in a particular woman. Believe it.

He's afraid he won't be able to hold a conversation...

For the man who uses this as an excuse for not calling a woman, I suggest you read a book and a newspaper — get a hobby, join a club. By doing this, you'd have something to talk about. It's that simple.

Jack
4 months ago
Scoff if you like Ms. Flowers. If these
techniques were ineffective, men would
not be doing them. Lavishing time and
resources on a woman who doesn't show
sexual interest is a fool's errand. To
you younger men posting here: You have 3
choices. 1) MGTOW out of the game. 2)
Learn Game. 3) Get a career path with a
high degree of mobility.

TTBone
37 hours ago
...LMAO men better start understanding
that we are the prize and that our time
is as priceless as these women believe
theirs is. MGTOW. Live your life for
you. Be your own man you don't owe
anyone anything. She needs to make equal
efforts to position herself in your
life. Most importantly, don't spend any
money on any woman until after the sex.

This article is really pathetic
10 months ago
Women fought hard to be treated like
men. Now that they are, they're upset
that they lost all the perks that came
from not being men. As a good-looking,
successful man all I can say is this:
Why in the F*** would I do any of the
above things? Women are sluts today. I
can walk out of my apartment and find a
girl to bang in under two hours on any
given week night. YOU did this, ladies.
YOU demanded sexual liberation. Okay

great! Now we men have all the sex we want. No commitment necessary... Marriage is dead and women killed it. And men do not need it and never did.

#1 Men don't accept rejection anymore

Overly sensitive...

I don't know if men just don't know how to take it or they've become more sensitive than they used to be, but they seem to be terrified of rejection. And this is partly the reason they don't do the things listed in this book anymore. And for the men who think women don't face rejection, yes, they do. Women are constantly rejected for not being thin enough, having hair that's long enough, not being pretty enough, etc. Again, gender roles are switching.

Take rejection personally when they shouldn't...

A man should step out of his feelings if a woman turns him down. Let's face it, sometimes rejection is personal, but mostly it isn't at all. Even if a woman doesn't see a romantic encounter brewing initially, doesn't mean she won't later. So, lighten up. Stop with the attitudes. Take it all in stride.

Instead of using it to build character, they become angry ...

Rejection is painful—for everyone. And out of pain comes anger. If people in general accepted the fact that most so-called rejection was not personal, it would be better for all of us. And, in general, people should understand that every *no* they receive gets them one step closer to the person perfect for them.

Jason
4 months ago
Good article, but it seems unfortunately optimistic for this era. Chivalry IS officially dead. Let's look at the sliding scale… One date is a couple of days of planning. A couple of hundred dollars for dinner and drinks, plus the flowers and/or gift. Now let's assume for a moment that I want to look presentable… dry cleaning and a car wash before I pick her up. And all of this is so that I can find out if she is interested? [There's an] old saying … "just because you bought me dinner, that doesn't mean that I owe you anything?" I believe the statement is correct. But, how about "just because I think you are interesting, doesn't mean that I owe you anything." If the interest is mutual, then let it blossom organically. If the interest isn't mutual, I'll save my two hundred dollars.

Arthur
2 hours ago
I'm 46 and never been married, never had a girlfriend and never had a date, had sex or been kissed. I've been rejected by every woman I've asked out from high

school onwards. At this point I've given up on it ever happening—what's the point? I don't know why nothing ever happened – none of my women friends have any idea either. I'm not a 'nice' (passive doormat) guy; I'm genuine, friendly and have a great sense of humor. My experience has shown that no matter what I do, I'm just not—and obviously cannot be attractive in 'that' way to any woman.

Finally

10 Things Women Could Do Better

The main reason that all of these things don't happen anymore is because women, at large, stopped requiring them. We've turned men into lazy daters and pursuers. You could argue that a guy is just not interested when he takes the short cuts, but that's not it alone. Even when he's genuinely interested, he doesn't have to call—he can text; he doesn't have to take a woman on a real date— today's woman accepts the meet-up; he doesn't have to take notice of her brains and compassion—they go unnoticed because of her blossoming and exposed cleavage and big behind. I have always declared to be a romantic while making it very clear, however, that I am not a hopeless one, but I really do wish we could just go back.

But, until then, here are 10 things women could do better:

10: Stop playing games.

If you aren't
interested in a
guy, let him
move on to the
next chick.

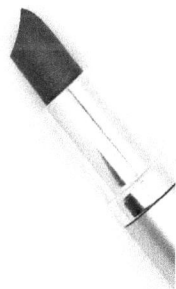

9: Do away with wanting her man to be a thug.

Learn to see guys who treat them well, and pay their own bills, as fun guys to be with.

8: Expect and receive chivalry with grace.

Embrace
it; you
deserve it.

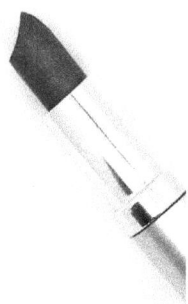

7: Make having fun
on a date her only goal.

Don't look any
further than the
next date, while
out on the
current date.

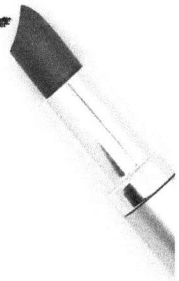

6: Realize her vagina is not special.

Have more to offer than world-class sex because the competition is stiff.

5: Stop being so thirsty.

Desperation looks good on no one.

4: Be kind without
lowering her standards.

There's no need
to be rude; if he
isn't for you,
politely send
him on his way.

3: Accept being
treated well by men.

simply extend
a genuine and
h e a r t f e l t
'thank you'.

2: Expect to be
treated well by men.

w i t h o u t
arrogance, set
expectations
for yourself.

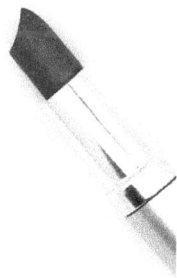

1: Love herself.

Learn to love
yourself so
you'll
you
recognize
loving acts
when they
come to you.

More From the Blog

Jason
3 months ago
Women are evil. If you get out and about, they absolutely will smear you. Many times I'm given evil eyes at random. I can be in a room with 50 girls, and they will make fun of you literally behind your back. You, author, make a list like this without any examination. If you think there's something wrong with men and felt the need to make a list, girl, I couldn't, not ever remotely, relate to you in any way, shape, fashion, or form. You're as good as alien. Our perceptions and life experiences couldn't be further away.

Chuck
5 months ago
How about this!!! Take away the fatties, narcissists, phone addicts, no makeup Earth chicks, bareleggers, ugly clothes, foul mouthed, no perfume, crappy sarcastic attitudes, money grubbers, un loyal, drama queens, tattooed, body modificationed, ugly complicated shoes then what's left? For what reason would a MAN want to date these foul women today? Then once you actually do date one you find all they do is ride the cock carousel! Not to mention being targeted for an unwanted pregnancy if you have any "value"! Bitter? Hmmm! Not only FEMALES can be bitter!

Jamie Smarson
4 months ago
Unfortunately Chuck, your response is
what feeds Elaine Flowers, and women in
general, to say all men are terrible. It
is a really annoying cliché, which
Elaine has attributed to all men
multiple times in her comments such as
above. I don't think we can close this
gender divide by simply hating the other
sex, which you and Elaine (is sometimes)
are doing…

L
2 years ago
Thank God for you, Elaine! This is SO
true! As for the men who have posted
about how women are ingrates or reply
with a "what is in it for me?" I agree
some things women should NOT expect such
as being bought a drink or for a man to
show up with a gift EVERY single time
you go on a date but others should be a
given! Such as asking a woman out,
making the plan in advance, and showing
initiative whether it be asking a woman
to dance, going on a date, or coming up
with a suggestion as to where you would
like to go! All of these demonstrate
interest and I am sorry is a must for
most women! We demonstrate OUR interest
in accepting your invitations! ...I
totally agree with the last comment if
you find a woman you like don't be
standoffish! You win some you lose some
but lord if you never try you will never
find out! She could be the one you were
destined to find but you let her walk
right out of your life!

Mr. Meanie
3 years ago
Dating expectations have been extremely lopsided in the woman's favor, but that's changing... Women are almost never expected to do any of the things listed in this article, and—surprise—many modern men don't want lazy daters, either! You'll have to forgive me if I don't have much sympathy for your frustrations.

Bob Smith
22 months ago
To the author of this article, you have GOT to be joking. This is a gag, right? Okay, I'm going to put on my best imitation of a whiny, complainy, woman's voice here for a minute: "Men don't ask us out anymore. Men don't compliment us anymore. Men don't bring us gifts/tokens at the door anymore. Blah, blah, blah, blah." Are you F***ING serious? Why don't you take a look at yourself and your girlfriends and see what YOU are doing or not doing that might be the source of your complaint.

Reg
6 months ago
We don't do these things 'cause you're not worth it anymore. Third-Wave Feminism has turned women into men. We'd rather be single. Stop bitching.

Sam
6 months ago
It's like narcissism, selfishness, solipsism, and entitlement had a weird, nasty four way and you're the result of it.

Winter
6 months ago
About number 3: Have you ever been to
bars lately? And have you read the news
about rapes or kidnappings when a woman
accepts a stranger's drink? And number
4: I still don't know why so many people
love modern dancing music … seriously, a
dog's barking has much higher quality
and the lyrics… a kindergarten book is
way smarter and more elaborate than that
pile of crap. That's why I don't dance,
people here only dance to that garbage
…(The ironic part [is] that the lyrics
usually insult women and most of them
dance to it so happily).

Jim
6 months ago
A guy can get laid without the effort
these days, so why bother with all the
things in your list?

BC
6 months ago
This is amusing. The title of this
article should have been called
"Delusional Entitlement." The "author"
has been reading too many romance novels
and watching her fill of daytime
television. Note the absence of any
mention of going Dutch or splitting the
bill. (Yes dear...Those are dates, too.)
Instead, it's all about what men can do
for women. She continues on about what
men could be buying for these takers.
Gift, presents, dinners, rides, movies
and offering to buy her drinks because
he's taking her valuable time like she's
actually doing him an incredible favor
by merely existing in his presence.

"Thank you, ma'am! May I purchase you an over priced fruity beverage that you won't finish with me anyway?" She doesn't want a man; she want's to date Santa Claus. ...And number 6? You're kidding right? Not only do we need to buy our way into your heart, but now we need to "impress" her too. Yes! We must prove we're "worthy" and manly enough for thy Princess… Good luck with the future. Consider cats.

goldielox2382
5 months ago
This. This. And, this again.

Mad hatter
6 months ago
Women are so unappreciative, all they want is a chocolate penis that shoots out money.

Late2theparty
6 months ago
Eh... Ever since I gave up on the illusion of ever being in a relationship life's been wonderful. It is so much easier to just look at porn. Variety, low maintenance, and easy access. Versus what? Drama, mind games, hypocrisy. LOL are you serious… WE'RE HUMAN BEINGS TOO. Men are not expendable resources… GROW UP. Don't play the game and then complain about the rules. Then once you change the rules, you complain again because we do what you should have done in the first place. Not play.

Ray79
7 months ago
I do all this stuff: planning dates, being well dressed, inviting, leading, and accepting rejection. Women just don't want average looking guys or guy who have normal life (a decent job, some friends and hobbies) they want "amazing" guys, extra social, great looking. At the end it's an unworthy invest in time and energy. I'm 37 y/o and I stopped looking at women anymore, I read a lot everywhere to avoid looking at them, I watch videos about science, war and SF movies, I avoid any "romance" thing and concentrate on my career, health and friends. Unfortunately, dating is dead because of women's hypergamy.

Steven B.
7 months ago
Yes, many men are now shunning women and literally blocking them out. It's getting serious out there in the dating scene and personally I don't like it. Not sure where things will go 5, 10, 20 years down the line for couples and the dating and marriage scene. Guess we'll have to wait and see.

Javier
9 months ago
I'm just not interested in really getting to know a woman. I guess I might be asexual now, which is weird because when I was younger I loved trying to get women to talk to me.

Megness
8 months ago
As a woman, I like that all of these things have changed.

Elaine FLOWERS

is a professional writer of mainstream fiction residing in Dallas, Texas. She became a published author in 2004 with the release of her *Dallas Morning News* bestselling novel, "Black Beauty" and went on to pen five more books, including one co-authored with Angela Germany, a book of date stories submitted by single men and women titled "So... How Was Your Date?"

Elaine's current book on the woes of dating titled, **"MGTOW: Ten Things Men Don't Do Anymore"** derived from her blog on dating in the 21st century.

Elaine holds a Bachelors of Fine Arts in Creative Writing for Entertainment from Full Sail University and is also an editor, publisher, and screenwriter.

Website: BooksByElaineFlowers.com

BeforeYouPublish Book Press™
—————— We Publish Books ——————
BEFOREYOUPUBLISH.COM

www.ingramcontent.com/pod-product-compliance
Lightning Source LLC
Chambersburg PA
CBHW071058040426
42443CB00013B/3366